Photo: iStock

CONTENTS

// PARENT GUIDES

Yvonne Hackett // CEO
yvonne@catalystanz.com.au

Eileen Berry // Editor
0407 542 655 // eileen@parentguides.com.au

Sarah Marinos & Cheryl Critchley // Writers

Anita Layzell // Art Director

Max Hunter // Production Editor

Julian Healey & Mary Riekert //
Social Media Editors

Michele Benson // Schools Liaison Officer
0419 311 315
michele@parentguides.com.au

Kimberley Barry // Marketing Director
0439 900 350
kimberley@parentguides.com.au

PARENTING GUIDES LTD IS A REGISTERED CHARITY
Website // parentguides.com.au
Facebook // www.facebook.com/parentguides
Twitter // @ParentGuidesAU

Every attempt has been made to contact holders of copyright for material used in this book. Parent Guides welcomes inquiries from anyone who thinks they may have a copyright claim.

TEEN USE

Young Australians go online to be entertained, to communicate, to search for information and to simply browse.

There's no doubt that teenagers live in a digital and highly connected world. In many households they are online from the moment they wake until they go to bed – or until frustrated parents confiscate their smartphones and tablets.

The latest statistics from the Office of the eSafety Commissioner and the Australian Communications and Media Authority show just how prevalent the online world has become in the day-to-day lives of Aussie teenagers.

The Aussie teens and kids online report found 82 per cent of teenagers had been online in the past four weeks – up from 74 per cent in 2011. Teenage girls and teens living in cities were more likely to be using the internet.

Around 83 per cent of teenagers go online at least three times a day and most are using their mobile phone to do so.

They are streaming videos from YouTube and TV – 64 per cent do this compared to 34 per cent in 2011. Research and browsing, sending emails and social networking are also popular online activities. Websites with videos, movies, games or music accounted for 56 per cent of teenagers' online browsing time, the report found.

The facts and figures make for interesting reading – and highlight how important it is for parents to keep an eye on what their children are doing online and where they are hanging out in cyberspace.

> Seventy-four per cent of parents worry about the online content their child might access.

SMARTPHONES AND SOCIAL MEDIA *

- Australian children generally get their first smartphone at the age of 12.
- In research for Telstra, 65 per cent of parents say they give children a smartphone so they can contact them when they need to.
- Seventy-nine per cent of parents surveyed worry that a stranger will contact their child online.
- Seventy-four per cent of parents worry about the online content their child might access.
- Thirty-nine per cent of parents believe social media apps on smartphones distract kids from study.
- Bedtime is also disturbed by smartphones, with 66 per cent of parents admitting kids use their smartphone between 9pm and midnight on a school night.
- Just over one million Australian teenagers aged 14 to 17 have a mobile phone. Of those, 94 per cent have a smartphone.
- The Australian Child Health Poll found almost all Australian teenagers, two-thirds of primary school children, and a third of pre-schoolers own a tablet or smartphone.
- Three in four teenagers and one in six primary school children have their own social media accounts.

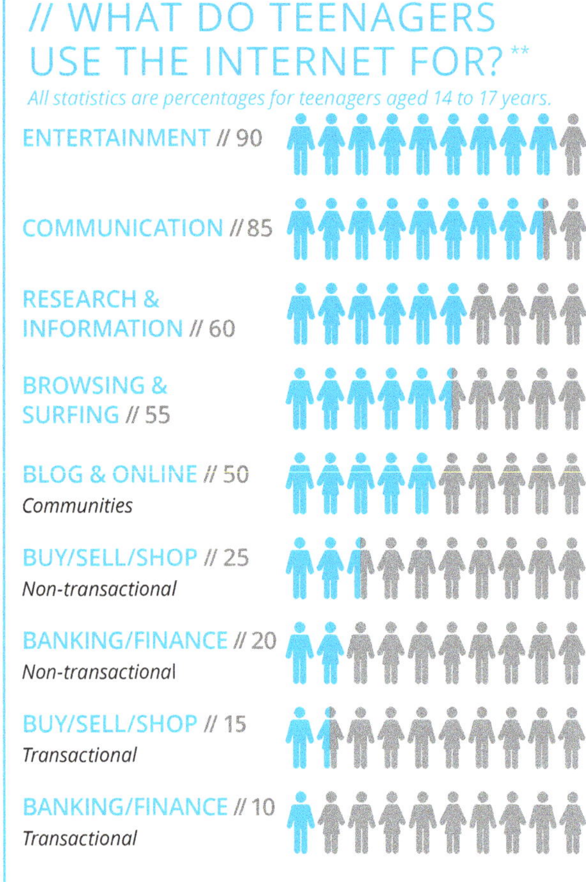

All statistics are percentages for teenagers aged 14 to 17 years.

ENTERTAINMENT VS SHOPPING

Teenagers are more likely to use the internet to entertain themselves – 90 per cent use it for this reason, compared to 75 per cent of adults who go online for entertainment. But adults are more likely than teens to use the internet to carry out transactions such as shopping, selling or banking.

- Teenagers spend the most amount of time on a screen-based device at home – around 44 hours per week. That's equal to having a full-time job. The six to 12-year-old age group averaged 32 hours per week. Parents averaged almost 40 hours per week.
- 68 per cent of parents with teens aged 13 to 17 believe their children spend too much time online.
- 28 per cent of parents with teens say they regularly talk to their child about spending too much time online.

* Source: Telstra and ACMA Aussie teens and kids online snapshot report, Roy Morgan Australia July 2015 Australian Mobile Owners research, Australian Child Health Poll (The Royal Children's Hospital Melbourne), Office of the eSafety Commissioner ** Source: ACMA Aussie Teens Online report – Nielsen Online Ratings. *** Source: Office of the Children's eSafety Commissioner for period covering April 2015 and Nielsen Online.

HOW DO AUSTRALIAN TEENAGERS ACCESS THE INTERNET?**

Teenagers aged 14 to 17 years.

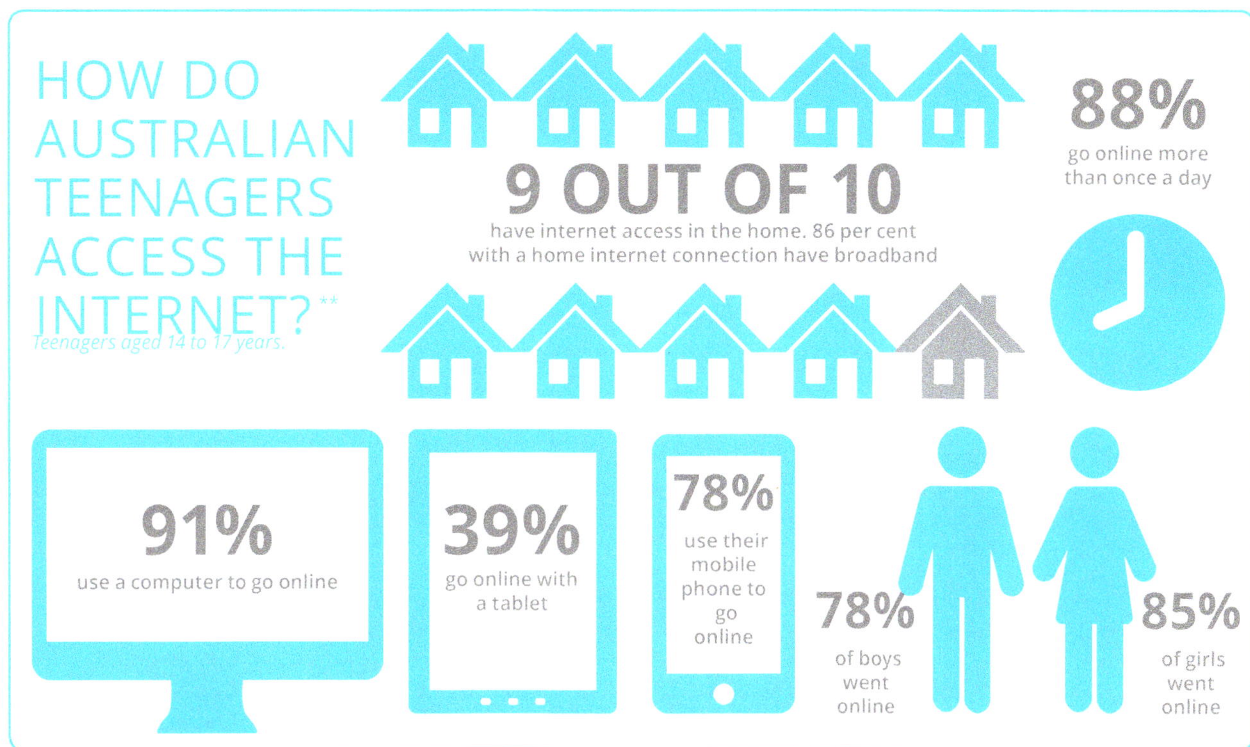

9 OUT OF 10

have internet access in the home. 86 per cent with a home internet connection have broadband

88% go online more than once a day

91% use a computer to go online

39% go online with a tablet

78% use their mobile phone to go online

78% of boys went online

85% of girls went online

// WHAT ONLINE CHANNELS DO TEENAGERS ACCESS AND WHEN?

TOP 5 ONLINE CHANNELS**

Percentage of teenagers who visit online channels.

GOOGLE	FACEBOOK	YOUTUBE	Mi9	MICROSOFT
77%	**53%**	**50%**	**49%**	**39%**

EACH CHANNEL IS AN UMBRELLA FOR A NUMBER OF SITES

Google // Google+, Google Search, Gmail, Chrome, Google Maps, Google Earth and other Google services and products.

Facebook // Facebook platform of profiles, pages, apps, games and associated websites.

YouTube // User-generated and professional media video content that can be viewed on the website, via apps or embedded in third party content.

Mi9 // nineMSN, the Nine Network, ACP magazines, Skype, Xbox and other Mi9 services and products.

Microsoft // MS Windows, MS Office, MS Download Center and a range of Microsoft devices and support services.

TIME OF DAY ONLINE***

Easy smartphone access means teens are online more often, across a broader range of times. From 2011 to 2015, the percentage online between 10pm and midnight almost doubled, and doubled from midnight to 7am.

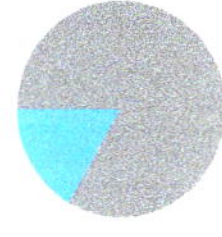
27% 07:00 - 08:59

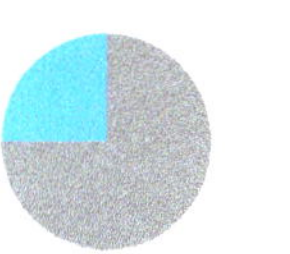
27% 09:00 - 11:59

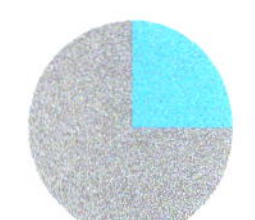
35% 12:00 - 14:59

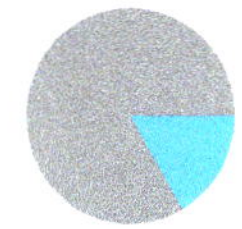
49% 15:00 - 16:59

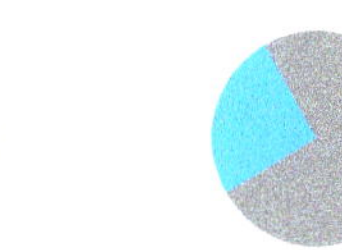
74% 17:00 - 19:59

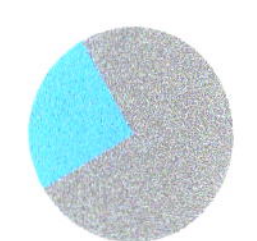
28% 20:00 - 21:59

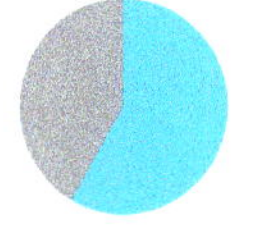
8% 00:00 - 06:59

// WHAT PERCENTAGE OF TIME DO CHILDREN SPEND ON DIFFERENT TYPES OF WEBSITES?***

Social networking† // 32 per cent
Games // 14 per cent
Videos, movies and music†† // 13 per cent
Consumer electronics, telecommunications and general commerce // 11 per cent

Education, careers and news // 9 per cent
Search engines // 5 per cent
Other // 16 per cent

† Includes YouTube †† Excludes YouTube

APPS & SITES

Do you know YouTube from Facebook? Or Snapchat from Instagram?

While there is talk of Facebook losing some of its appeal for teenagers – mostly because they feel too many parents have invaded the social media site – it's still the most popular online meeting place site for teenagers. About 71 per cent of them share photos and use Facebook to find out what friends, and friends of friends, are doing.

Instagram and Snapchat are also popular channels for today's teenagers and their user numbers are on the rise. They're the place to share candid moments, share videos and photographs, make a statement or send quick messages – 20 per cent of teens use Instagram and at least one in 10 uses Snapchat.

YouTube is also a long-time favourite of children and has more than a billion users worldwide. Year on year, the number of hours people spend watching YouTube content increases by 50 per cent and 300 hours of video are uploaded to the site every minute.

Here we give you a brief summary of the most popular social media apps that you have probably heard of, and some that you may not be as familiar with.

JAMES // 15

WHAT'S YOUR FAVOURITE APP? Facebook.

WHAT DO YOU LIKE ABOUT IT?
I can stay in touch with friends who I'm not at school with and don't see regularly. And it keeps me in touch with friends who live out of Melbourne. I also use it to buy and sell clothes.

WHAT APP DON'T YOU LIKE AND WHY?
Snapchat worries me. When you send a photo or video with Snapchat, it doesn't only go to the person you want to send it to – it goes into a file and is saved by Snapchat. During a social-media workshop at school recently I was told that 83 per cent of Snapchats that are sent are saved somewhere where they could be hacked. I don't think it's safe.

WHAT OTHER APPS DO YOU LIKE TO USE?
Instagram and Minecraft.

// POPULAR APPLICATIONS

AGE 13+

PHOTO SHARING
Instagram is all about sharing photos and short videos. People can upload their own material, share it with friends, view images and post comments on material shared by their friends and people they follow. About 95 million photos are shared every day, and about nine million Australians a month use Instagram, according to Social Media Statistics Australia (December 2018).

Instagram's default setting for all photos makes them available for viewing by anyone using Instagram. It's a good idea for children to create a private account instead, so only people who follow them, and whom they know, can see their images.

A Help Center with a Privacy and Safety section has instructions on how to ensure photos and videos can only be seen by people approved by your child to follow them. It also shows how to block people.

Instagram has an 'Add to Photo Map' feature where a location can be added to a photo and reveal where it was taken. This is usually turned off but once it is turned on, it stays on until it is turned off again. Encourage teenagers to think carefully about sharing details of where they are – especially if their account settings are public.

A comprehensive Tips for Parents section at Instagram Help Centre is at **help.instagram.com**

Hot tip from Project Rockit // Use the DM (direct message) feature to support someone having a tough time // **@projectrockit**

AGE 13+

PHOTO MESSAGING
Snapchat is a media-sharing and chat app. The text, photos and videos your child sends automatically disappear between 1 and 10 seconds after posting. Over 180 million people use Snapchat every day, and about 6.4 million Australians use it each month. While 'Snaps' are supposed to be momentary, they can be screenshot, which may leave images open to being used or shared in a way your child didn't intend. Talk to teenagers about ensuring that any images they share won't embarrass them or get them into trouble.

Look at Privacy Settings to make sure teenagers only receive images from people they know.
- Filter who can send you Snaps by tapping the ghost icon at the top of the camera screen to access your profile.
- Then tap the gear icon in the upper-right corner to reach the settings menu.
- When you see 'Who Can Send me Snaps', choose 'My Friends'.
Inappropriate content can be reported. Press and hold on the Snap, then tap the Button with the flag emblem.
For help, go to // **support.snapchat.com/a/privacy-settings**
Go to // **support.snapchat.com** for safety advice and how to report concerns and abuse.
Snapchat lets you to block someone from sending you Snaps // **support.snapchat.com/a/block-friends**
You can delete your teenager's account at **accounts.snapchat. com/accounts/delete_account** You need the username and password. If a teenager won't reveal them, parents can file a deletion request at **tiny.cc/5fsj8y**

VIDEO SHARING

At its most basic level, YouTube is a video-sharing website. It is designed for users aged 13 or older. YouTube has over one billion users. Every day people watch over a billion hours of video and generate billions of views. 15 million Australians use YouTube each month according to Social Media Statistics Australia from (April 2019).

YouTube does set out some basic rules for users. Videos featuring nudity or sexual content should not be posted, nor should violent and graphic content be shared. There is a flagging feature on video and if you see content that is offensive or concerning, you can flag the video and submit it to YouTube staff for review. That content may then be removed.

Go to YouTube and log on to the Safety Center for parent resources. This provides information about what kind of content is not allowed, reporting and includes tips and tools on how to stay safe and screen out disturbing content **support.google.com/youtube**

You can also visit your child's channel to see what they are posting and what they are watching on YouTube.
Go to // **www.youtube.com/yt/about/policies/#community-guidelines**

PHONE MESSAGING

WhatsApp is officially described as a 'cross-platform mobile messaging app'. Essentially, it allows you to send and receive messages without paying SMS fees. More than one billion people in more than 180 countries, including around seven million Australians, use WhatsApp.

Users can set up groups to receive messages from each other and to send images, video and audio messages.
There is a block facility, so messages sent from a blocked contact won't be delivered. Your online information and status message updates won't be seen by blocked contacts either. But blocking someone won't remove their contact from your WhatsApp list. To delete them you must delete the contact from your phone's address book.
Go to // **www.whatsapp.com/faq** for details about the app and safety options.

SOCIAL NETWORKING

Facebook is a social networking website where users create a profile, upload photos and videos and send messages.

About 1.56 billion people use Facebook every day. About 15 million Australians check in each month (Social Media News, May 2019) and around 940,000 are aged between 13 and 17.

Facebook has ramped up its 'community standards' content monitoring, focusing on adult nudity and sexual activity, bullying, harassment, child nudity, sexual exploitation of children, fake accounts, hate speech, regulated goods, spam, global terrorist propaganda and violence and graphic content.

The latest metrics from May 2019 suggest that for every 10,000 times people viewed content on Facebook, 11 to 14 views contained contend that violated the company's adult nudity and sexual activity policy, and 25 violated its violence and graphic content policy.

Children should check their privacy settings so they know who is seeing their content. They should click Account at the top of any page and then Privacy Settings in the dropdown menu. This means they can control who sees their posts, limit the audience of posts they share with friends of friends, and limit who can send them a friend request.

It's important to control who can see your profile contact info. Go to your profile and click the Update Info button. Look for the Contact Info section and then click Edit.

Use the audience selector at the right of each piece of contact information to adjust who it is shared with.

Facebook has a Family Safety Center with safety resources and general safety information // **www.facebook.com/help/**

Hot tip from Project Rockit // Challenge online hate in risk-free ways. For example, write a 'counter-comment', i.e. type 'dislike' and use your status to take the power back // **@projectrockit**

MESSAGING SERVICE

Twitter keeps people in touch with short messages, photos, videos and links. Posts or 'Tweets' are sent to followers once you click the 'Tweet' button. Twitter sees free expression as a human right and aims to give everyone a voice. But Tweets cannot be abusive or threatening and the company has a suite of features to keep Twitter safe. About 4.7 million Australians use Twitter each month.

You can mute an account to stop seeing Tweets from someone without blocking them and you can block words, hashtags and phrases. You can instantly block an account and opt out of images that you don't want to see. Parents can use the 'safe search' function to remove potentially sensitive content by default. **@TwitterSafety** keeps users up to date with the latest safety updates and tools.
Go to // **help.twitter.com**

MORE APP CHAT...

We explain other apps your teenager may be using regularly

AGE 13+

MEDIA MANAGEMENT

iTunes was created by Apple and can be used to play and download music, music videos, TV shows, movies, audiobooks, podcasts, apps and ringtones on computers, iPhones and iPads. Children have to be at least 13 years old to have an iTunes account.

iTunes is set to be replaced with new Mac apps for music, TV and podcasts. Until then, parents can stop children from being able to install or delete apps and make in-app purchases on iTunes.

- Go to Settings and tap Screen Time.
- Tap Content & Privacy Restrictions.
  Enter the passcode if needed.
- Then tap iTunes & App Store Purchases.
- Then choose a setting and switch it to 'Don't Allow'.

You can also limit the content children can access, such as blocking music with explicit content, preventing movies and TV shows with certain ratings and stopping children from accessing apps you'd prefer them not to have access to.

- Start with Settings and tap Screen Time.
- Then tap Content & Privacy Restrictions and Content Restrictions.
- Choose the settings you want under Allowed Store Content.
  You can also restrict access to games, such as multiplayer games.
- Go to Settings and then Screen Time.
- Go to Content & Privacy Restrictions and then Content Restrictions.
- Find the Game Center and then choose the games you wish to restrict.

Apple Support is at **support.apple.com**

If you have a Family Sharing arrangement set up with iTunes, parents can also turn on the Ask to Buy feature. This applies to family members under the age of 18. When your child wants to buy something from iTunes or download a free item, a request is sent to the person in control of the Ask to Buy feature. You can then check the request and either make the purchase or refuse it. If you go ahead, the purchase will download to your child's device. If you refuse it, no purchase or download will happen.

Go to // **www.apple.com/au/support/**
Family sharing // **www.apple.com/au/icloud/ family-sharing**

WHAT'S YOUR FAVOURITE APP?
Instagram.

WHAT DO YOU LIKE ABOUT IT?
I like to use it to talk to my friends and I like to see the photos they upload. It lets me see what my friends are up to and keeps me up to date. I look at photos more than I upload though – I usually only upload photos if I'm at a party.

WHAT APP DON'T YOU LIKE AND WHY?
I wouldn't use Facebook. I don't think there's enough privacy and I'd worry about strangers accessing my private information.

WHAT OTHER APPS DO YOU LIKE TO USE?
I use Jacaranda to do my homework.

** Parent authorised*

SOCIAL NEWS

Google is a search engine that scours the Internet for information. Reddit's tagline is 'Conversation starts here' and the social news internet site is used by millions of people worldwide who share comments, views and interests. The most interesting posts and comments are 'upvoted' to the top of the pile or the 'Hot' pages. About 330 million people use it every month and take part in chats and forums that match their interests – called subreddits. Subreddits range from Parenting and Politics to Comics, 'Today I Learned' and Gaming.

Earlier this year Reddit raised $300 million in investments which will be used to improve and streamline the website.

// USEFUL TIPS FOR PARENTS

ConnectSafely.org is a US-based not-for-profit organisation that aims to educate people about how to use technology safely. The website has lots of safety tips, research and guides for parents on how to keep children safe when they surf the internet and use social media.

Useful guides that can be downloaded include *A Parents' Guide to Mobile Phones*, *A Parents' Guide to Instagram*, *A Parents' Guide to Cyberbullying* and *A Parents' Guide to Cybersecurity*.

Go to // **www.connectsafely.org to download the guides and for practical safety tips.**

SOCIAL NETWORKING

AGE 13+

Pinterest started in 2010 as a place for people to collect ideas they found around the internet. It's about getting inspiration from other people's ideas and what they share. Pinterest now has an international community of more than 250 million people and is home to more than 200 billion ideas.

The Help Center has information on how to best manage an account and to maintain privacy. For example, if you want to block a Pinterest user, open the profile of the person you want to block. Then click on the flag symbol. Click block and then OK to confirm. To unblock an account, open the profile of the person and then click unblock. **help.pinterest.com**

TikTok

AGE 12+

VIDEO SHARING

TikTok is described as 'the world's leading destination for short-form mobile videos'. Using smartphones, people capture and share moments of their everyday life. In 2018, TikTok was one of the world's most downloaded apps.

TikTok produces a Community Well-Being series with information on how users can make the most of various safety and privacy tools. Some of the key tools are being able to keep your list of liked videos private by going to Privacy and Settings – click on the three dots in the top right corner. Then go to 'Who Can See the Videos I've Liked' and choose between All or Me.

Users can keep the videos they make themselves private by choosing 'Private' on the video posting page where it asks, 'Who Can View This Video'.

By default, initially TikTok accounts are public – so you need to actively switch to a private account. Parents can get advice on safety for children on TikTok at **support.tiktok.com**

DID YOU KNOW?

TINDER // Fifty per cent of the dating app users are 18 to 24 years old.

SARAHAH // "Kids are using this to bully other kids. There's no way of telling who they are so they think they can say anything. My 13-year-old daughter had a deluge of sickening abuse and sexual harassment. I've deleted it off her phone." Parent review on Google Play

SOPHIA // 10

WHAT ARE YOUR FAVOURITE APPS?
Stick Cricket 2 and FIFA.

WHAT DO YOU LIKE ABOUT THEM?
I like playing cricket and soccer and you can have multi-player games and compete with other people.

WHAT APP DON'T YOU LIKE AND WHY?
I don't like Talking Angela – it's boring. I don't like Instagram because I don't like the idea that lots of people can see your photos. I don't think that it is very safe. I don't like sharing my private photos and private information online. I worry about my accounts being hacked so I just don't bother with those kinds of apps.

WHAT OTHER APPS DO YOU LIKE TO USE?
I like sports-related apps like Real Boxing and ESPN.

AGE 13+

MICRO BLOGGING

The Tumblr app is a blogging platform where people can post short texts, photos, quotes, links, music and videos. About 3.7 million Australians use Tumblr.

In December 2018, Tumblr introduced new Community Guidelines around the type of content that can be shown on the site. Content flagged as 'adult' is no longer allowed. Tumblr defines adult content as 'photos, videos or GIFs that show real-life human genitals or female-presenting nipples, and any content – including photos, videos, GIFs and illustrations - that depicts sex acts.

Tumblr accounts are generally public and, according to antivirus and security company McAfee, a primary Tumblr account is always public. But you can start a secondary blog or account and protect it with a password to be more private.

Tumblr also has an 'ignore' feature that blocks people you don't want to communicate with from being able to see your blog posts. Nor can they send you messages or follow your blog and your blog won't appear in their search results. To block someone, open your blog, go to the user menu and select 'Block'. For help with security concerns about Tumblr, go to // **www.tumblr.com/help** or visit **support.tumblr.com**

MUM // **iPhone 8 Plus, laptop, iPad**

7am	Turns phone and laptop on. Checks emails and works while the kids prepare for school/uni.
8am	Works on laptop.
11am	Calls a friend to arrange a catch-up.
12pm	Eats lunch while checking Facebook/Twitter.
3pm	Another quick check of Facebook/Twitter.
6pm	Dinner while watching TV.
7pm	Emails friends to arrange catch-up.
8pm	Takes daughter to netball. Checks emails and Facebook while watching.
10pm	Tells younger two to turn off devices for bed and charge in the dining room.
11pm	Plays Scrabble on iPad for five minutes and falls asleep.

DAD // **Samsung S6 phone, laptop**

7am	Drags kids out of bed and makes their lunches.
9am	After dropping kids at school, onto the laptop for work.
11am	Checks AFL Super Coach team status on phone.
1pm	Eats lunch while scrolling news on the phone.
3pm	Checks emails on laptop.
5pm	Cooks dinner.
6pm	Dinner while watching TV.
8pm	Ensures 16-year-old is doing homework on desktop.
10pm	Tells 18-year-old to remove iPod and phone from her bedroom.
11pm	Checks emails and Super Coach on laptop before bed.

MODERN FAMILY

Meet the our generic family and their kids.

Some parents admit defeat when it comes to teenagers accessing the internet 24/7. But you may be able to control their time online, even if they sneak an iPhone or iPad into their room late at night.

Many teenagers have pre-paid phones or limited phone data. This means they may rely on their parents' Wi-Fi for the devices they use at home, including phones, iPods, iPads and laptops. If so, you can control this use. Most routers, which generate the home's Wi-Fi signal, can be switched off. This kills the signal for the whole house.

Parents can do this at a certain time each night to ensure that everyone is offline. You can also use your router to control Wi-Fi use on individual devices or groups of devices.

Through your router, you can specify when a particular device and/or user will be online or not. For example, you can turn a 12-year-old's laptop and iPod off from 8pm-7am, and a 16-year-old's laptop and iPad from 10pm-6am. You can also filter out certain websites, such as porn and gambling sites, using key words.

EXTRA HELP

If unsure how to do this, ask a tech-savvy friend. Or Google "how to access your router online".

Each router has its own unique (IP) address that you can access via an internet browser on your laptop or iPad. Once you access the page, it should have a parental control section that allows you to control internet access on all your home devices once you have registered them.

NOTE // These methods don't work on phones using external data.

DAUGHTER // 20

Laptop, iPhone 8 Plus, iPad

7am	Gets up, checks messages on phone.
8am	Takes phone and laptop to university.
11am	Checks phone messages between classes. Texts mum to ask if she can book concert tickets.
1pm	Eats lunch while checking phone messages. Texts mum to ask if she got the tickets.
3pm	Checks messages and listens to music on the train. Texts mum asking what row the tickets are in.
4pm	Homework on the laptop.
6pm-10pm	Works at a fast food restaurant.
10pm	Drives home.
11pm	Checks messages before going to bed.

// GIRL UNPLUGGED

At 15, Keira Baker didn't have Facebook. Or Instagram. Or any other Social Media. OMG.

// The physio digs her thumbs into the crook of my shoulder. 'So when you're sitting on the computer at home on Twitter or Facebook, you can do these neck exercises. This physio has immediately made the presumption that because I'm a 'teenager', I obviously spend all of my time huddled in a dark room over a phone or laptop screen.

"Just like teens in movies, I must also be grumpy and messy and moody and rebellious, desperately besotted with social media, and give my 'totally loser' parents massive eye-rolls. (I am pretty good at eye-rolls, actually, but only for sarcastic use.)

"The truth is, I'm 15 years old – but I'm not really a 'teenager'.

"I don't have Facebook, Instagram, Twitter or Snapchat. In fact, the only form of social media that I have is Edmodo – a lame kind of 'educational Facebook' where you can receive school assignments and feedback. And even this I can't use because I somehow managed to translate the whole site into Spanish. (I'm not the most technologically inclined.)

"If my phone buzzes, it will be my mum saying, 'No, you can walk home!' and the majority of my messages come from Optus or are weird call-centre promotions.

"I guess there are plenty of reasons why social media is great – keeping in touch with old friends, messaging people, organising things and providing a brilliant opportunity to share millions of horribly unnecessary photos.

"I'm not avoiding it to be cool. I'm not making a stand against conformity or trying to be 'alt-y' (alternative) and fashionable. I don't have any social media because … I just don't want it.

"Not having Facebook or Instagram doesn't have a huge impact on my social life. It does mean, however, that my friends really are just that – friends.

"I don't interact with anyone unless I'm comfortable with inviting them over for a swim or going out to the movies.

"Occasionally, I do miss out on something. Our school drama class is organised on Facebook – so all the assignments, notes and reminders about our productions are put up there. My friends are pretty good at letting me know if there's something important (and some less important things: 'OMG, you have to see this cat meme'), but every now and then I'll come to class in school uniform while everyone else is dressed as a '50s housewife/ghost/robber for a performance.

"One terribly sad side-effect of social media is the replacement of the phone call. Birthday mornings used to be busy with calls from family and friends and strange aunts you never even knew existed.

"Now on my birthdays, I pretty much only get called by my grandparents – and although waiting on the line while my grandpa hums a tuning note for his annual operatic version of *Happy Birthday* can be somewhat awkward, it sure is nicer than getting a 'hve a gr8 bday' message from some distant friend who only sent it because Facebook reminded them to.

"Probably the best thing about not being a 'screenager' is that I don't have an online persona to keep up. I don't have to worry about which photo is pretty or cool or beachy or alt-y enough for my profile picture. I don't have to build up a social-media identity and showcase the things I want other people to see in me. I can be whoever I want to be without worrying about how many 'likes' that photo gets.

"And perhaps that's the reason I don't have social media. Simply put, I don't want to have that pressure to be fake.

"So maybe next time I'm at the physio I'll correct her. Explain that no, my neck problems aren't from hunching over Facebook or Instagram. And I'm not a 'teenager' either. I'm 15 years old and a perfectly capable human being."

To read the full article visit // **www.dailylife.com.au/dl-people/girl-unplugged-20150616-ghphq1**

WHAT YOU NEED TO KNOW ABOUT GAMING

Did you know 97 per cent of Australian homes with children have computer games?

In September 2015, a Russian teenager addicted to online gaming died after developing suspected deep-vein thrombosis. The 17-year-old had spent 22 consecutive days playing popular online game *Defense of the Ancients*.

He collapsed and died after developing a thrombosis, like those that passengers can suffer on long-haul flights. In the 18 months leading up to his death, investigators say the teenager spent about 6.5 hours a day playing online. During the days preceding his death, he had broken away from his computer screen only to eat and nap.

While this case may seem extreme, online games present another potential challenge for teenagers and parents, who need to become familiar with what their child is playing online, and with whom they are playing.

A 2018 report from the Office of the eSafety Commissioner found eight in 10 young people aged eight to 17 played games online in the 12 months to June 2017. The same report found online multiplayer gaming is very popular, with six in 10 young people playing these games.

Many online games include content and themes unsuitable for certain age groups. So games often come with age recommendations or ratings, similar to movie or film classifications. For example, *Call of Duty (CoD)* has an MA 15+ rating and contains strong themes and violence. *Clash of Clans*, a multiplayer game, is recommended for players over the age of 13.

Many games allow players to communicate through forums, chat and messaging services. In the interests of player safety, Activision, creators of *CoD*, recommend young people never share their password or give players they meet online their name, address, email address or school details. Computers and tablets should also have up-to-date security software to protect against viruses.

Supercell, owner of *Clash of Clans*, does not pre-screen or monitor all user content and recommends that players never share their login data or log into their account on someone else's device.

Parents should also be aware that some games allow players to purchase points, different versions of the game and game-related merchandise. The Office of the eSafety Commissioner found around 34 per cent of eight to 17-year-olds made an in-game purchase in the 12 months to June 2017. So find out whether your child is using money to play online.

The Office of the eSafety Commissioner lists a number of games and has comprehensive information on game content, who can play, how to protect personal information, how to report cyber-bullying or abuse and how to block your child spending money while playing online.

Go to // **www.esafety.gov.au/esafety-information/games-apps-and-social-networking** // **www.videogames.org.au** // **www.instituteofgames.com**

Watch // **www.abc.net.au/7.30/content/2015/s4472277.htm**

RISK FACTORS

- Withdrawn
- Nightmares
- Loss of interest
- Online friends vs real friends
- Anger about not being able to play

Find out more // **internetsafeeducation.com** // **familyzone.com** // **eSafety.gov.au**

Photo: iStock

GAMING AND YOUNG PEOPLE: A SNAPSHOT

76% of children under 18 play video games.

60% of parents play online games with their children in the same room.

81% of parents are familiar with controls on online games.

84% of parents say they have discussed playing safely online with their children.

48% of parents say they play online games with their children as a way of spending time with them.

77% of parents say they have rules about how long children can play games.

76% of parents have rules about games their child can play.

Digital Australia Report 2018 by Interactive Games & Entertainment Association

WHAT YOU NEED TO KNOW ABOUT FORTNITE

This game has been one of the most popular video games for children and young people in recent times. The free version, *Fortnite: Battle Royale*, operates across Windows and Mac, Xbox and PlayStation. However, while the game itself is free, players can purchase outfits, weapons and other accessories to boost their chances of survival. *Fortnite* pits players against other players around the world and the aim is to be the last person standing on a sometimes violent and hostile island inhabited by monsters and enemy figures. On average, each game can last around 20 minutes, assuming your character doesn't get killed before that. The Australian Council on Children and the Media says *Fortnite* is not recommended for children 12 years and under. Parental guidance is recommended for children aged 13 to 17.

INTELLIGENT GAMING

Andrew Kinch is founder of GameAware. He says video games – in the right measure – can help young people meet some important psychological needs.

"Gamers have been stigmatised over the years. There used to be a time when people wouldn't admit to their friends that they played video games. Once an underground subculture, in 2017 these games were a $109 billion industry.

"Gamers often feel the need to become defensive when they're told that their passion is a waste of time. After that, anything that is true about the harms of excessive gaming is completely ignored. It's a polarised debate between those who play and those who blame video games as the cause of gaming disorders. The truth lies somewhere in the middle and is often complex.

"Gaming is a great form of entertainment, but we must be on top of our self-regulation skills, especially when the motivation to play is to escape real life. When gaming becomes a coping mechanism to seek relief from pain, it can become excessive and problematic. People can choose gaming to attempt to meet their needs. When you combine this with easy access and the game mechanics that entice players to keep coming back, you can see how an individual might be motivated to live in the virtual world.

"In my experience, video games hit three motivational needs for young people: competence, autonomy and relatedness.

"Competence is the feeling of mastery. Everyone wants to be good at something and video games allow you to become good at something quickly. If I want to be good at basketball it can take years – with video games, it takes months and you do it without breaking a sweat.

"Secondly, teenagers and children don't have a lot of autonomy in their lives. In a game, they have freedom over their own choices and can express themselves creatively. They can customise their characters and develop a second identity if they choose.

"Every multi-player game meets the third need, which is relatedness or social connection. When you play with other people – in a competitive or collaborative way – you feel part of something bigger than yourself. You are part of a gamer

Photo: Supplied

community. Gaming can allow kids to build self-confidence because the community is accepting of people from all walks of life and any age.

"I'd argue that you can't completely fulfill psychological needs through video games. Real life will always provide us with the opportunity to feel more fulfillment from competence, autonomy and social connection."

THREE THINGS YOU CAN TRY NOW

1 Do a 10-day gaming challenge – go cold turkey and stay away from games and gaming culture.
But parents can't just yank the Wi-Fi. It must be something the gamer decides to do to test the commonly spoken phrase – "I could stop if I wanted to, I just don't want to". The challenge is about helping a gamer help themselves. Even if they don't reach 10 days, you get information as to whether they can control themselves. However, three or four days in to the challenge, gaming's grip tends to be loosened!

2 Parents need to play video games with their kids.
Get coached and get a better understanding of the nuance in the games your child plays. Be a spectator from time to time to show interest. If you take your child to soccer and watch them play, they feel valued and it's the same if they see you are taking their gaming seriously. Take down defensive walls by getting involved. The conversation about gaming changes when parents are not considered the opposition.

3 Set up social gaming sessions to be shoulder-to-shoulder with friends.
When we game in the same room and play the same game, the dynamic is more exciting and provides a level of connection that online gaming isn't quite able to provide.

Andrew Kinch is founder of GameAware and developed Intelligent Gaming strategies to keep gaming healthy. www.gameaware.com.au

GAMBLING ONLINE

Dr Wayne Warburton says statistics suggest that in most high school classrooms in Australia, one teenager would have a gambling problem.

"Studies of Australian youth gambling show 3 to 4 per cent of teenagers have a problem – in adults it's around 0.5 to 1 per cent of the population. It seems teenagers are more susceptible to problem gambling, but it's not an obvious problem.

"Most parents wouldn't know their teenager had a problem because teenagers tend to be very reluctant to admit to gambling – it's illegal under the age of 18 and teenagers don't want to get into trouble either for gambling or for the ways they may have obtained the money to gamble. They may also feel ashamed and not want their social network to know just how many people they have borrowed from.

"For many teenagers, a gambling problem begins online with an activity that isn't strictly gambling but gets them in the mindset to gamble. Look at the pop-up banners and the games you can play on many social media sites that are simulated gambling.

"Those online games are programmed to make you win – it's almost impossible to lose. They groom you to believe you are going to win a lot of money, that you are skilled at it, and this sets up gambling behaviour.

"Typically several of the top 10 iPhone gaming apps are casino-style games. You can spend as much as you want, but because they don't involve winning money, they're not 'gambling' so are unregulated. We know that kids access these sites and apps, and also play online video games that have a gambling component. Many games have gambling-like devices to progress, skins that can be gambled online or loot boxes that can be purchased. Interestingly, loot boxes were recently shown scientifically to have most of the same characteristics as gambling. Research also suggests that making in-app purchases for gambling-like activities is predictive of developing a gambling problem later.

"Parents need to know about gambling apps and simulated gambling and to realise that for some kids this will be a precursor to developing a gambling problem. The companies that sell these products wouldn't be doing this unless it had a payout. It's big money and a big industry.

"For some teenagers, gambling becomes a bigger part of their life and school becomes less and less important. Gambling becomes more important than friendships and family and teenagers often start to lie about money and what they are doing with their time. Teenagers don't have access to large amounts of money so they may steal from parents, buy and sell things illegally, or use a stolen credit card.

"On a practical level, parents can keep electronic devices in public areas of their home as much as possible. Use internet blocking devices that block pop-ups and invitations to gamble from coming up on screen. You can use internet monitoring software, although your teenager won't think that's very cool!

"Because children/teenagers are reluctant to talk about gambling, even when they're in financial difficulty and are scared that their gambling is out of control, parents need to know how to talk with a teenager about it.

"Keep the conversation open. Talk about the traps but don't be judgmental. Explain that playing gambling-like games online and making in-app purchases increases the risk of developing a gambling problem. Educate them about the inflated win-rate of such games and the low chances of success in real gambling – the odds of winning a poker machine jackpot are 9.7 million to one. They have a greater chance of being struck by lightning ('just' 1.6 million to one). Help kids understand that these online games and apps are designed to suck them in – and they do a really good job."

Photo: Supplied

// REMOVE TEMPTATION

POPULAR INTERNET GAMBLING FILTERS
- GamBlock
- Betfilter

INTERNET MONITORING SOFTWARE
- CyberPatrol
- CYBERsitter
- Net Nanny

BETTING IN SPORT
Psychologist Jo Lamble shares some tips for starting a conversation:
- Make use of stories
- Learn how to listen so your children will talk
- Choose the right time
- Use some humour
- Tailor your message to their interests
- Leave them wanting more

OTHER HELPFUL RESOURCES
Australian Council on Children and the Media app reviews with clearly labelled gambling information // **childrenandmedia.org.au/app-reviews/**
KidBet // **kidbet.com.au**
Gambler's Help Youthline (24/7) // **1800 262 376**
Gambling Help Online // **www.gamblinghelponline.org.au**
Parent resources // **www.responsiblegambling.vic.gov.au**

// Dr Wayne Warburton is an Associate Professor of Developmental Psychology at Macquarie University.

THIS IS OUR 'OH S..T' MOMENT

"The violations of loyalty, dignity, trust. The jokey video gone viral — and your child is the butt of the joke. The boasty pictures of the party your child isn't invited to; all the worlds the gatekeepers won't let them enter. The child whose friend asks for their password because, well, they're friends; then the Facebook page or Instagram account has been taken over by someone who mightn't have their best interests at heart. The embarrassing photo meant for one person's eyes only, posted online for everyone to see. The urging of your child to go kill themselves and do everyone a favour. And some do.

"It's the underbelly of our children's screen-saturated lives; a shadowy world we parents often don't know about. But many of us witness the changing child and feel queasy. The tiny heads bowed. The curiosity sapped. The spark of brimful life lost. The aggressive tantrum when a screen is taken from them and they become someone else.

"There's been talk recently that this young generation's addiction to social media and screens is akin to smoking cigarettes in the '60s – no one knew of the dangers they were sailing into, no one saw it coming. And now, all around us, are rumblings of concern about kids and screens and it feels like a vast cottoning on. Yes, it's great babysitting, but at what cost? What are we doing to them?

"Earlier this year two large Apple investors urged CEO Tim Cook to issue health warnings for children using iPhones. They want the technology behemoth to examine the impact its products are having on young people amid growing concerns over the smartphone's connection to mental health – psychologists believe we're setting ourselves up for a public health crisis.

"In Australia there have been calls for the introduction of the online equivalent of apprehended violence orders. Children need to know that cyber-bullying has consequences, not only for others but themselves. Too often it's 'other' kids doing the bullying. It's just too easy to do. Cyber-safety charity the Carly Ryan Foundation wants police to be granted powers to ban cyber-bullies from social media for sustained periods of time; to put young people on notice and give them the chance to do the right thing; to make them pause, and think. Because children, if caught, would be unlikely to reoffend. There's a huge shame factor there.

"The federal government recently announced that kids as young as four would now be given lessons in cyber safety; police have noticed that children are posting explicit images and being groomed online at shockingly young ages.

"An Auckland school recently asked parents to ban their children from using social media for the two years they're there. Kowhai Intermediate School declared: 'We believe it would be highly beneficial for our students and indeed families to create and support a social media-free community for students outside of school hours.' They're all in this together.

"The recent suicide in the Northern Territory of 14-year-old Dolly Everett shone a spotlight on the issue. Dolly's 15-year-old friend, Katelyn Simpson, received vile Snapchat messages after her death, 'Why don't you just go cut your wrist until you bleed out," one urged. 'You'll do everyone a favour. Go do what Dolly did it should've been you not her'.

"It feels like we're in the midst of a massive 'oh s..t' moment. If kids are doing this, imagine what type of adults they'll grow up to be. Schools need to step up. Principals and counsellors. But most importantly, the parents. Engage more with what our children are involved with on screens: supervise, pry, question. Whether the kids like it or not."

> "There's been talk recently that this young generation's addiction to social media and screens is akin to smoking cigarettes in the '60s — no one knew of the dangers they were sailing into, no one saw it coming."

Photo: Adam Knott/ Random House Australia

CYBER-BULLYING

Federal and state laws exist to protect potential victims and punish offenders.

Cyber-bullying is illegal, but working out what aspects are covered, and how, can be a challenge. Cyber-bullying and its related offences are covered by a range of state, territory and federal laws. Some jurisdictions have specific anti-bullying laws, while others use existing laws to prosecute cases. Regardless of whether a jurisdiction has specific cyber-bullying laws, related behaviours such as stalking, making threats and physical assault are generally covered by existing state and territory legislation.

// FEDERAL LAW

ENHANCING ONLINE SAFETY FOR CHILDREN ACT 2015

Passed in early 2015, the Enhancing Online Safety for Children Act established a Children's eSafety Commissioner, a complaints system for reporting cyber-bullying material aimed at an Australian child and a two-tiered system for rapid removal of cyber-bullying material from large social-media services.

In 2017 the role was expanded to include all Australians and under the revised Enhancing Online Safety Act 2015 is known as the Office of the eSafety Commissioner. The independent statutory office within the Australian Communications and Media Authority (ACMA) administers cyber-bullying complaints, promotes online safety, co-ordinates relevant Commonwealth department, authority and agency activities, conducts and oversees educational and community awareness programs, makes grants and advises the Communications Minister.

A person can lodge a complaint to the commissioner if they have reported the material to the specific social-media site first and did not receive an outcome. The commissioner has the power to investigate complaints into cyber-bullying and conduct investigations as he or she sees fit.

Among other things, the legislation provides for:
- Setting out the eSafety Commissioner's functions and powers;
- A complaints system for cyber-bullying material;

Photo: Thinkstock

// SOUND ADVICE

Unbullyable by Sue Anderson can be purchased online.
Australia's Youth-Driven Movement Against Bullying // **projectrockit.com.au/about** or call 0435 150 280.
Body image movie *Embrace* //
www.youtube.com/watch?v=__2AayArYfs
Reach out // **au.reachout.com**

- A two-tiered scheme for the rapid removal from large social-media services of cyber-bullying material;
- A mechanism for the commissioner to give end-user notices to require a person who posts cyber-bullying material to remove the material, refrain from posting further material or apologise for posting the material; and
- Enforcement mechanisms.

Many forms of cyber abuse could be considered illegal under state or federal legislation. For example, under the Commonwealth Criminal Code Act 1995 ('the Act') it is an offence to menace, harass or cause offence, using a 'carriage service'.

It is also an offence under the Act to use a carriage service to make threats to kill or cause serious harm to a person, regardless of whether the person receiving the threat actually fears that the threat would be carried out.

These provisions could capture instances of menacing, harassing or offensive conduct and threats carried out using landlines, mobile phones (e.g. MMS, SMS) and the internet, including emails and social media. For example, using a mobile phone to repeatedly send offensive images to someone.

Most Australian states and territories also have laws covering stalking, blackmail, criminal defamation and various unlawful uses of technology. A number of jurisdictions have also passed laws creating offences for the threat to distribute, or distribution, of intimate images (image-based abuse).

Office of the eSafety Commissioner // **esafety.gov.au**

THE PROCESS FOR REPORTING CYBER-BULLYING FOR UNDER-18s

- Collect evidence
- Report to the platform/site in which it occurred
- If not removed within 24 hours, then report to the Office of the eSafety Commissioner

More info // www.esafety.gov.au/complaints-and-reporting/cyberbullying-complaints/i-want-to-report-cyberbullying

CYBER-BULLYING AND THE AUSTRALIAN FEDERAL POLICE

- Due to the internet's borderless nature, unwanted contact, harassment or cyber-bullying can occur from anywhere.
- Schools and parents should become involved in the first instance, as they would with most "offline" bullying.
- Schools should have a cyber-bullying policy with sanctions for students who bully others during or outside school hours.

Photo: Thinkstock

- Serious cyber-bullying or stalking cases can be reported to the Australian Cybercrime Online Reporting Network (acorn.gov.au).
- Through initiatives such as ThinkUKnow, the AFP works with state and territory police forces, Neighbourhood Watch Australasia and the private sector to educate about staying safe online.
- The AFP's High Tech Crime Operations Crime Prevention team presents at schools, junior sporting clubs and community groups about online risks and staying safe.

More info // **www.thinkuknow.org.au**

// THE AUSTRALIAN CYBERCRIME ONLINE REPORTING NETWORK

Cybercrime can be quickly and easily reported online. The Australian Cybercrime Online Reporting Network (ACORN) allows secure online reporting of online crimes. The Commonwealth, state and territory governments policing initiative also helps people to recognise and avoid common cybercrimes.

ACORN educates and advises about common cybercrime, such as hacking, online scams, online fraud, identity theft and attacks on computer systems, and advises victims. It also covers stalking and cyber-bullying, which can be reported to ACORN if the actions are intended to make the victim feel fearful, uncomfortable, offended or harassed. Those being physically stalked or concerned about their safety should report to local police immediately.

Those being physically stalked or concerned about their safety should report to local police immediately.

Cyber-bullying or stalking involves someone engaging in offensive, menacing or harassing behaviour using technology. It can happen to people at any age, time and often anonymously. Examples include:
- Posting hurtful messages, images or videos online;
- Repeatedly sending unwanted messages online;
- Sending abusive texts and emails;
- Excluding or intimidating others online;
- Creating fake social-networking profiles or websites that are hurtful;
- Nasty online gossip and chat; and
- Any other form of digital communication that is discriminatory, intimidating, intended to cause hurt or make someone fear for their safety.

More info // **www.acorn.gov.au**

VICTORIA POLICE

Simon Fogarty's working day is dedicated to reducing cybercrime, including the grooming and sexual exploitation of children via the internet.

"Generally, there are two types of offenders. There's the offender who has a scattergun approach who doesn't necessarily care about the age of the person they talk to via social media. They'll ask where someone lives, what they're wearing and then do they want to meet up for sex? Children may not be targeted specifically, but unfortunately they do get caught up in this.

"Then there is the offender who targets kids because of their age, and that is when we see the longer-term grooming process. Conversations start through social-networking sites, then offenders take kids to more private sites where they can have one-on-one engagement and develop a relationship.

"They start to get control over the child and usually convince a child to send pictures of themselves in various naked poses. When they have those pictures they use those photos to blackmail the child to send more pictures, or to meet up with them for sexual activity. That's known unofficially as 'sextortion'.

"Police do a lot of work within social-media sites. We identify who the offenders are, what they are doing online, and investigators then arrest and prosecute them. We do a lot of work with counterpart agencies interstate and overseas and we spend a lot of time researching where kids are accessing social-network sites and identifying child victims. It's a priority to find kids who are being exploited online and to rescue them.

"These kinds of social-media crimes are a growth area and they are under-reported. Kids can be unlikely to report an incident because they're worried about losing access to the internet or they're afraid or embarrassed.

"We've got to pull our heads out of the sand and realise this is happening to kids from all backgrounds. Parents need to take an interest in what their children are doing online and to talk to them about where they hang out and what is happening online. Build your child's confidence so they can approach you if they get into harm online because kids don't have the capacity to know how to get themselves out of danger.

"If your child does have problems online, call Crime Stoppers or go to your local police station. Contact the appropriate website administrator and make a report. There are also Sexual Offences and Child Abuse Investigation teams who we work closely with to investigate these types of crimes.

"We are interested in finding out what has happened online even if someone doesn't want to pursue an incident. Keep messages and images and a copy of the chat between your child and the potential offender. We may need access to your child's social network profiles – we only need their login details and can access their account at the police station.

"Look at the apps your child is using and learn how they work. You don't have to be experts but look at your child's iPad or mobile and see what they're doing online. But of course children need some privacy, particularly when they are older, and it's important they learn how to engage through social networks because that's the way of the world now. They may talk to each other in ways that parents think are a little inappropriate and we have to be flexible. But that has to be balanced with appropriate behaviour and your child's online safety.

"Our children need to understand that they wouldn't walk down a street with photos of themselves and hand out those and their phone number to strangers. Yet they get online and provide personal information to people they don't know."

For parents, carers and teachers // **www.thinkuknow.org.au/site/**

> "Our children need to understand that they wouldn't walk down a street with photos of themselves and hand out those and their phone number to strangers."

Photo: Supplied

// Simon Fogarty is a tactical intelligence officer with the Joint Anti Child Exploitation Team (JACET) – a Victoria Police initiative.

THE PSYCHOLOGIST

Are all teenagers sexting? No, says Brett Lee, who investigated child exploitation for 16 years, and says it is vital to understand that most teens do not sext.

// If a young person believes everybody else is sexting – and they're not – then they think they are missing out on something, that there must be something wrong with them, and if everyone else is doing it, it must be OK. A young person doesn't have the knowledge to allow them to make an informed decision that best protects them.

"Don't assume most teenagers are sexting. It's not 'normal' behaviour. But between the ages of 12 and 17 young people are looking for their identity and exploring where they fit and there can be a need or vulnerability. They want to be accepted – can't wait to grow up – and they may have someone in their life and think they must do this otherwise they'll lose them. Young people don't get involved in sexting for sinister reasons.

"In most instances, when young people sext, they are committing criminal offences and it can lead to embarrassment, humiliation, depression, fear, loss of dignity and blackmail – 'I'll make sure everyone at your school sees this photo unless you do this or that'.

"Parents don't have to know everything about the technology. Real world analogies are more important. I use an example of picturing yourself in a mall with thousands of people around. As you look through the crowd, you see someone you like – maybe you know them, maybe you don't. You push your way through the crowd, walk up to that person and take off all your clothes. Or that person says, 'take off your clothes' and you do that.

"When I watch the students' reaction I know they're thinking 'why would you do that? I'd never do that!' But sexting is similar. They take a photograph of themselves in a split second, share it in another split second, and it goes into a community of 3 billion people for the rest of their lives.

"Have conversations about the internet being public and discussions about whether your child would be happy for other people to see them naked. Ask them, 'if you send one of those photos and it became public, would you want to take it back if you could? How would you feel if your grandma saw it? What if you sent that photo to a friend and they left their phone on the kitchen bench, and your friend's Mum or Dad picked it up?' Verbalise real world outcomes so your child can consider them and it can sit in the back of their mind.

"A parent will be repaid for the rest of their life if they develop a culture of communication with their child about this. So your child knows you are interested and a source of support if something happens. If you think something is not right, step in and ask questions. Maybe you need to remove your child's device for a while until a situation is fixed – some parents feel it is a birthright for their child to have possession of their personal device. It is not. Technology is way down the list when it comes to what is best for our children."

Photo: Supplied

BRETT'S FIVE SAFEGUARDS

1 **Set rules and boundaries.** These are not optional.

2 **Stay current.** Increase your knowledge base as needed.

3 **Take charge.** You are the one who controls technology and makes the final decisions.

4 **Use Management Controls.** Parents have a right to know where their children go and whom they communicate with.

5 **Communicate.** Create an environment of openness about technology and talk about it with your kids.

www.internetsafeeducation.com

// Former Queensland police officer Brett Lee is the founder of Internet Safe Education. www.internetsafeeducation.com

eSAFETY TIPS

Whether your child is the victim or the bully, help is never far away.

// FINDING CYBER-SAFETY HELP

Hundreds of websites and organisations offer help and advice for parents. A great starting point is the office of the eSafety Commissioner website – a central portal for cyber-safety information and resources for parents, schools and children. Cybersmart resources, previously available on the Cybersmart website, are available through the eSafety Commissioner website (www.esafety.gov.au), as well as a complaints system to report cyber-bullying material targeted at Australian children.

The eSafety Commissioner also investigates illegal and offensive online material.

Online help and complaint links can be found at // **www.esafety.gov.au** or call Crime Stoppers on 1800 333 000.

HOW MANY KIDS ARE CYBER-BULLIED?

In June 2014, the federal Department of Communications released research that indicates that 20 per cent of 8 to 17-year-olds in Australia were cyber-bullied in a 12-month period. They are also more likely than non-victims to experience impaired social and emotional adjustment, poor academic achievement, poor physical health, low self-esteem, anxiety and depression.

WHAT DO GOOD ANTI-CYBER-BULLYING PROGRAMS INCLUDE?

Good school anti-cyber-bullying programs teach social skills and online etiquette with individual learning plans. They keep parents informed of, and involved in, cyber-bullying-prevention policies and prompt effective bystander behaviour by encouraging children to support others being victimised. It is important to establish a common language for discussing bullying and victimisation with young people so it has meaning to them. Involving young people in school policy development that encourages pro-social behaviour and bystander action is more likely to attract their support. Students must also understand that everyone has a right to feel safe at school and home.

COMMON MISTAKES BY PARENTS

Some parents overreact when their child is cyber-bullied and may remove access to technology, which can put children off confiding in them. Research suggests that children are less likely to tell adults about cyber-bullying if they think the adult will make things worse.

Parents should talk to their children about what cyber-bullying looks like before it happens and that it is not OK. They can plan what they will do together if it occurs. Parents should also make it clear that they will not tolerate their child cyber-bullying and encourage them to avoid negative conversations of any kind.

STAYING UP TO SPEED

Parents should learn about the technology that their kids use. They don't need to be experts but must understand what happens on the relevant sites, apps and games, whether the content is appropriate, what safety features they have and complaint mechanisms. Parents should walk through apps and websites with their child, checking age guidelines, looking at content, being honest about their feelings about it and giving the child their say. Open communication can protect against the impact of bullying and help put off potential bullies.

Parents sometimes don't check age guidelines for games, videos, websites and apps. These should be followed, regardless of what other parents allow. Don't be afraid to stand your ground. Many parents of younger children do not limit the Wi-Fi access of the apps and games, leaving children open to contact from others, which they may not be mature enough to manage.

Resources // **www.esafety.gov.au/parents**

> Good school cyber-bullying programs teach social skills and online etiquette with individual learning plans.

// WHAT IF YOUR CHILD IS THE BULLY?

Don't overreact, but have consequences. All children make mistakes and need a chance to repair their errors. A calm conversation is likely to have more impact than a heated argument, even if parents need to wait a day or so until they have calmed down. It is helpful to raise the target's feelings, to help the perpetrator understand the hurt caused and help prevent a reoccurrence. It is important not to become extremely angry with your child, despite your disappointment, as you need to model forgiveness and empathy for them to develop the social skills needed to prevent future bullying.

Photo: Thinkstock

// eSAFETY TIPS FOR PARENTS

YOUNG CHILDREN

- Closely monitor their internet use;
- Know how your child uses the internet and explore it with them;
- Teach them to tell a trusted adult if they feel uncomfortable about something they see;
- Have rules about what sites are appropriate, what is appropriate to post and telling a trusted adult before posting any personal information;
- Teach them online manners and to ignore and report negative messages;
- Consider filters and other tools to manage online access;
- Install and update anti-virus and other esecurity software; and
- Seek professional help if your child shows concerning changes in behaviour or mood.

OLDER CHILDREN
As well as the above general tips …

- Talk to your child about personal information and how it can be used to locate them. They should never share passwords;
- Keep computers in a shared or visible place;
- If they use social networking, help them sign up safely, use privacy settings and decide how to choose "friends";
- Consider getting them to use avatars or usernames that don't identify them or provoke unwanted attention;
- Encourage them to use the same manners online as they would offline;
- Monitor their use and be alert for signs of overuse;
- Discuss cyber-bullying before it happens and have strategies prepared in case it does;
- Encourage them to report concerns to you;
- Discuss cyber-stalking and online grooming and encourage them to report any concerns to a trusted adult; and
- Educate them about their online reputation, e-security and appropriate downloading.

TEENAGERS
As well as the previous tips …

- Stay involved with their use of technology and ask them to show you what they use and the sites they visit. If they agree, ask them to help you set up your own accounts to see how the sites work;
- Encourage them to use social-networking site privacy settings so that only their friends see their material;
- Remind them to create screen names that are not sexually provocative and do not reveal their gender, age, name or location;
- Encourage them to think before they post and ask themselves who might see or misread it;
- Ask them to think about images they upload of themselves to ensure they aren't risking or compromising their own or others' privacy;
- Advise them to keep online friends online and not meet unless in a public place during the day, possibly with a trusted adult;
- Encourage them to ignore negative messages, block abusive people, report them to site administrators and tell a trusted adult;
- Help them block and/or report bullies;
- Reassure them that you won't block their internet access if they are bullied;
- Encourage them to support friends involved in cyberbullying; and
- Advise them to check links sent through social media before clicking.

THE PSYCHOLOGIST

Professor Helen McGrath, of the National Centre Against Bullying, says there is no such thing as 'safe sexting'.

"Sexting is usually used to describe the sending of images of yourself in states of undress, and it's something young people are doing and keeping from parents as they explore their sexuality. They are trying on risk within their environment, as they do with alcohol, for example. It's also part of identity formation – young people are developing an interest in romance, sexuality and relationships and figuring out how they engage in sexual interplay with another person.

"But technology has created more potential for harm and there is no such thing as safe sexting. The first risk is that young people get in way over their heads. Suddenly they can be sexting someone they don't know very well, and once they send sexual images of themselves to someone else, those images are no longer theirs. Anything can happen to those pictures.

"It's common for young males to show off images they receive to their mates – 'look at what X sent me'. So when someone tells your child that only they will see that image of your daughter naked, what they really mean is that only myself, my best friends and their best friends and their mates will see it.

"And the person your child has sexted may try to exploit and bully them by demanding money or threatening to send images to more people. So your child arrives in year 9 or year 10 at school and everyone is giving them knowing smirks because they've seen those photos.

"There is also the risk of strangers in chatrooms soliciting pornographic images and then disseminating them. So someone pretends to be a 19-year-old male in a chatroom, communicates with your child for a few weeks, and then requests naked photos. Really that person is a 52-year-old man collecting pornographic images to sell to other people.

"Sexting is not a new risk per se. Young girls and boys have always been potentially exploitable in regards to other people using them for sexual satisfaction while pretending to negotiate some kind of relationship. It's just that sexting make this easier and it can be more lethal.

"Sexting opens the door to revenge, misuse and exploitation because of the nature of the images. So parents need to give children a message that sexting is never a good idea, but without being sensationalist.

"Talk to your child about having ownership of their body, of images of their body and of their sexuality. If you self-respect, then you self-protect – help your child understand that they need to protect their reputation or 'brand'. Your child doesn't want to go for a job at the age of 22 and have those images of them still floating around.

"We know companies do internet searches of potential employees and they have private-investigation firms that do that kind of research for them. If sexting-type images come up,

Photo: Supplied

employers can assume your child doesn't have a good reputation and doesn't have a sense of risk management. Things your child does now – like sexting – have an impact on their brand and go with them for life.

"You need to show your child that you understand their situation. Tell them that you probably see us as doddery old parents but we were young, too. There were sexual risks when we were around. I remember being in high school and a boy said the 15-year-old girl he was going out with was having sex with him. I don't actually think that was true but the same week that he spread that rumour, three or four other boys in school hit on that girl on the grounds that if she was doing it with one boy, why not others? This kind of behaviour isn't new, but now it is less containable.

"Parents can explain that they are not saying don't have sexual engagement, but know that sexting is a high-risk activity and, as with drugs, some people take drugs and escape unharmed but a lot more people don't escape unharmed – and it's the same with sexting. You can send an image to your boyfriend or girlfriend and maybe they won't send it on – but they may. And when that happens, it's vicious."

....

// Professor Helen McGrath, of the National Centre Against Bullying, is a psychologist.

DIGITAL NUTRITION

What is 'digital nutrition'? Jocelyn Brewer says we can take the same approach to our intake of digital content as we do when considering what and how we eat food.

"We talk a lot about digital addiction and digital detoxing – terms that are very negatively framed. That doesn't sit well with me because the future is going to involve technology. We need to embrace the kinds of skills we need to use technology in a clever way.

"I coined 'Digital Nutrition' as a response to the idea that technology is toxic. There are decades of research and public education on healthy food and eating choices and Digital Nutrition borrows from that. It emphasises the importance of balance in the way we use technology but also in considering evidence of its impacts.

"When you have the basics of a healthy, balanced relationship with technology, you don't need to force yourself offline to find peace. If it's school holidays and it's raining, your kids are more likely to spend more time online. At Christmas, we eat and do things in excess and in January we make resolutions about eating healthy again.

"Some research says playing things like Candy Crush for 20 minutes at the end of the day is a great circuit breaker – it helps people chill out and decompress after a day's work. But that is different to playing for 90 minutes when you haven't had a conversation … it's about context.

"And Digital Nutrition is positive about the opportunities that technology offers modern communities.

"We get obsessed with 'digital calorie counting' – we're stuck on measuring screen time and using that as a measurement of impact. But we need to look beyond that to what people are consuming. Young people may be looking at Instagram but is that content making them think 'I'm not pretty/good/smart enough' – or are they on Instagram following inspiring and aspirational people?

"If there was a nutritional label on technology and games and apps, what would be the vitamins and mineral content, and what would be the fats and sugars? Look for virtual vitamins, like Vitamin E for empathy. When kids play a certain game, are they sharing the experience of the other person in the game? Are they seeing new perspectives? Look for games and apps with plenty of Vitamin C for Creativity – do they create and contribute something, rather than consuming, consuming, consuming?

"Because these nutritional labels don't exist, parents need to play the games and use the apps and social media that their children are using. And teens and kids need help to think about whether they want a particular app or game to be a snack or a sometimes food, rather than their main digital meal. As in real life, you don't want to eat hot chips all the time …

"If you are someone who loves chocolate and can't have it in the fridge because you'll eat it all, be aware of this temptation from a digital perspective, too. Just like not being able to stop at one or two squares of chocolate, if you dip into something online do you then lose a sense of time? If so, maybe you need to take that app off your phone, just like not keeping chocolate in the fridge."

> "Playing things like Candy Crush for 20 minutes at the end of the day is a great circuit breaker."

THE THREE Ms OF DIGITAL NUTRITION

Mindful // Pause and think more broadly about how what you do, say, click on and scroll through affects your overall wellbeing.

Meaningful // Have a sense of purpose and clarity in what you read, comment on or participate in.

Moderate // Use technology in moderation. Also consider moderating what you say and how you react to things that show up in your online world.

Photo: Supplied

// Jocelyn Brewer is a psychologist and former high school teacher who developed the concept of Digital Nutrition. She is part of Australia's first formal cyber-psychology research group at the University of Sydney. www.digitalnutrition.com.au

THE LAWYER

If your son or daughter does something offensive on social media, what's the potential legal fallout? Katie Miller highlights some of the legal issues.

Photo: Supplied

// "The key thing to remember about social media is the same rules apply in the online world as apply in the offline world. So the same kinds of things that get children into trouble offline get them into trouble online.

"But social media and the online world have changed the game by making everyone more connected, and so allowing potentially problematic situations and actions to happen more quickly. For example, bullying that would happen at school over a term can now happen 24 hours a day, seven days a week. So the groundswell can build more quickly and the effects can be longer lasting.

"But we wouldn't accept our kids being bullied or bullying offline. And while bullying online may cause psychological rather than physical harm, that doesn't mean it's acceptable. If your child is saying nasty things about someone else online, theoretically that could be defamation.

"When it comes to the online world, know what your kids are doing online and talk about their responsibilities. It's not a lawless world. Just as there are rules in the physical world, there are rules to comply with in the online world.

"Explain to kids that often rules on social-media websites are about protecting them and so many sites state that children should be over the age of 13 to join. But parents sign up younger kids because kids pester parents that all their friends use that particular site and parents relent. But when you sign up your 10-year-old to a social-media site that's for children aged 13-plus you're sending the message to your child that online rules don't matter.

"When it comes to mobile phones, children under 18 can't sign a mobile-phone contract, so when you sign that contract for your child you have an important role to play in ensuring your child understands the boundaries of the law and how to use their mobile responsibly.

"Sexting is a key issue that parents need to know about. Sexting generally starts between two consenting teenagers as an extension of flirting behaviour. The problem can arise when that relationship goes bad. Then one person decides to distribute intimate photos of their ex, or in some cases a person uses intimate photos of another person to intimidate and threaten them.

"Until very recently, teens who took intimate photos of another person, even when they were engaging in consensual sexting, could be considered by law to be creating child pornography.

> "When you sign up your 10-year-old to a social-media site that's for children aged 13-plus you're sending the message to your child that online rules don't matter."

That's a problem, because if you're found guilty of creating child pornography you become a registered sex offender.

"In Victoria the law recently changed to ensure that young people who engage in non-exploitative 'sexting' don't end up with a criminal record on the sex offenders' register. But if your teenager distributes intimate photos of another person without their consent, i.e. the wounded boyfriend sends intimate photos of his ex-girlfriend as revenge, then they are committing a crime.

"Ultimately, if you have confidential information from someone – an intimate photo or something they've told you online – and you spread it further than the sender intended, that could also be a breach of privacy.

"Always remember that you sign the mobile-phone contract for your child. So if you suspect that your child is using their phone inappropriately you can talk with them about that, but at the end of the day if they don't listen then you pay for the phone, you sign the contract, you own it – and you have options.

"Keep reminding children that there is nothing special or different about the online world and the real world. Talk to them about what is right and wrong and what rules apply, and make it clear that if they break the rules there are consequences within the family, at school, and perhaps with the police and the courts.

"Look at your own behaviour with social media, too. How do you treat rules online? Children copy their parents, and if they see you treating online rules as flexible and breakable, don't be surprised when they do the same thing."

// Katie Miller is immediate past president of the Law Institute of Victoria.

THE PRIVACY EXPERT

Dr Suelette Dreyfus says while parents need to stay in touch with how their children use the internet and social media, making the right decisions online is a skill.

I had a conversation about children and their online presence years ago with Julian Assange, my co-author of Australia's first mainstream book about computer hacking, who was also a father. He said if you tell your teenage boy 'you can't have free run on the internet because there are bad things out there and you might see those things', the first thing he will do is hunt down the 'forbidden fruit'.

"His point was that parents are often better off explaining and reasoning with their teenager rather than just forbidding access to information. His approach at the time could be described as 'I trust you to be responsible using the internet. Yes, there are some bad things online, but there is also a big, bright world at the other end of that ethernet cable. If you want to do something interesting and valuable with your life, explore that world'.

"Parents need to work out where their child sits on the spectrum of freedom versus constraints, wisdom and maturity. If a teenager is generally truthful, have regular discussions with them about what they're doing online and set parameters with them. But you don't need a heavy-handed sniffing of the network to monitor all their traffic approach because reading every text message is unrealistic. The minute you take off that harness, they may lash out. You also don't want them to live a double life you don't know about because they feel constrained.

"The kind of rule that is sensible is that their circle on social media needs to be closed. I've put constraints on my children that it only includes friends they know face to face – not friends of friends and tenth cousins once removed! There must be a relationship in the real world that generates accountability that improves behaviour online.

"If teenagers are spending a lot of time alone in their room, it's reasonable to ask to see their messages. Explain that it's not so much about the content but finding out what is eating at your teenager emotionally. Seeing what they are doing online is not only about protecting them from creepy people – just as serious is recognising depression.

"Technology allows children to isolate themselves more. If you get enough information about what is worrying them, go online and find resources. A great gift of the internet is that people who would otherwise be outsiders can find a community of people just like them. Helping them make appropriate use of specialist communities can make a teenager feel less isolated in their awkward years.

"In terms of what they place online, ask your child to remember how incredibly uncool they were in grade 5. That's how they are going to feel in year 12 if they do stupid things online today. You can talk about it hurting their chances with employers later, but they won't get that – but they understand embarrassment.

"People don't necessarily want privacy because they are doing anything wrong – they want privacy because it's a kind of autonomy. It allows us to make mature choices in deciding how much information about ourselves we are going to give someone else.

"That decision-making and recognition that there are different pieces of ourselves that we do or don't want to share is part of becoming independent. Parents need to give their teenagers a chance to practise that. We don't hand the keys of an undriven car to an 18-year-old who has never been behind the wheel and say, 'Off you go! Good luck!' We do an awful lot of test driving first, and it's the same with learning to manage privacy.

"Privacy is a basic human right, and if your child knows this they feel they have some power. This lets them own the outcome of your discussions so they are more likely to abide by it.

"Finally, if you think your child will never find out that you're monitoring them online, think again. If and when they find out, that breaks their trust in you."

Photo: Supplied

// Dr Suelette Dreyfus is a lecturer in the Department of Computing and Information Systems at the University of Melbourne. Her research interest is in privacy and anonymity.

STAY IN CONTROL

A range of tools can help parents control their child's use of social media.

To the uninitiated, cyberspace can be a bewildering world. And at first glance, the social-media landscape can be an unfamiliar and unfriendly place where parents seem to have little ability to monitor and control how their teenager operates.

So where do parents start if they want to gain a better understanding of what their children are doing online? What effective and easy-to-use resources are available to support concerned families? What actual tools can parents use right now, and what practical steps can they take, to become informed about how their children are using social media?

The good news is that parents aren't powerless when it comes to having influence over their child's social-media use and experiences. The resources and tools available to parents can help them control how often and how much time their children spend using social media, and what kind of online content teenagers access. And parents don't have to become IT experts either.

> Parental controls aren't a silver bullet and they won't block all inappropriate content.

// SOCIAL MEDIA SECURITY SETTINGS BIBLE

Facebook // Access "Privacy Check-Up" by clicking on the question mark on your Facebook tool bar. Under "Your Posts" select "Friends", "Only Me", or "Custom" to choose who you want to see your posts. Then click "Next" and repeat for all categories. When done, select "Finish".

Instagram // Click on the person icon and then the Setting Icon. Scroll down and turn on your "Private Account" setting.

Twitter // Click on your profile picture in the top right corner, then click on "Settings and Privacy". Click on "Privacy and Safety". Turn off "Find Me By Email". Turn on "Protect My Tweets" and switch off "Receive Direct Messages From Anyone".

Snapchat // Head to Settings, click through to "Who can contact me" and select "My Friends". Then back in the Settings tab, click through to View "My Stories", click on "My Friends" or "Custom" to choose who sees your images.

Note // These instructions are for laptop versions. Phone versions may differ.

// PARENTAL-CONTROL SOFTWARE

WHAT ARE PARENTAL CONTROLS?

Parental-control tools help parents to monitor and limit what their children do and see online. There are many tools available and they offer different functions, such as allowing parents to limit the amount of time children spend on certain websites or games.

Currently, there are more effective tools for use with PCs and Macs than with mobile, tablet devices and game consoles. The important thing to remember is that no tool is 100 per cent effective at blocking access to inappropriate content online.

WHAT DO PARENTAL CONTROLS DO?

Most control tools allow parents to block children from accessing specific websites or apps, and they filter inappropriate material, such as sexual or violent content.

Most parental controls also allow parents to monitor their child's online activities by reporting on the sites that children access, the length of time spent on those sites and how often your child accesses them.

Parents can use controls to set time limits and so block their child's access to game sites or to social-media sites after a set period. Additionally, many parental control tools allow parents to change the "tool settings" according to a child's age, i.e. you can control who sees your child's posts on Facebook, who can see their images and profile, and control and tighten their privacy settings.

DO PARENTAL CONTROLS BLOCK ALL THE BAD STUFF?

- Parental controls aren't a silver bullet and they won't block all inappropriate content, but they can reduce the chances of your child being exposed to something they shouldn't see.
- Currently, parental-control tools are more efficient at blocking "adult" or sexual content than content that may promote self-harm, eating disorders, violence, drugs, gambling, racism and terrorism.
- While new control tools are being developed every few months, at the moment some may have difficulty filtering content within social-media sites and messaging services, including video-messaging services such as Skype.
- Parental-control tools are improving on game consoles, mobiles and tablets.
- Parents still need to keep talking to children about what social-media sites, games and apps they are using, who they are communicating with and what kinds of material they are accessing.

// CHOOSING THE BEST PARENTAL-CONTROL TOOL

So how do you decide what tool is best to help protect your child online?

Parental-control tools are developed and updated regularly, but the most effective tools are the ones that are easy to install and use. User reviews are a good guide to helping you find the right tool. Look for a tool that:

- Allows you to monitor your kids' online behaviour without them knowing, and has the ability to schedule monitoring times and password access;
- Blocks content and websites. Blocking and filtering elements may include application blocking, chat blocking, search-engine filtering and social-network blocking;
- Offers good reports on which websites have been accessed and computer use. This should include screenshots, keyboard strokes and online searches. Some products can capture usernames and passwords for sites such as Facebook;
- The best parental-control software will capture screenshots and send you emails about activity on your child's computer so that you stay informed, even if you are far away;
- Is automatically updated to ensure new websites and content are blocked;
- Can be used remotely – handy if your child is doing a school project and the tool is over-blocking content, or if children are home alone and you want to know which websites they are visiting; and
- Is compatible. In a household it is likely that you will want to monitor a number of computers and phones with different operating systems. The best parental-control software is compatible with a range of phones and operating systems.

FINDING THE BEST PARENTAL-CONTROL TOOL FOR YOU

Look at recent reviews on trusted consumer review sites and technology review sites such as TopTenReviews, TopConsumerReviews, *PC Magazine* and *Laptop* magazine. You can also search for the latest reviews on parental-control tools, content filters and internet filters.

Remember that parental controls don't provide software or hardware security. For this you need firewalls to block access by unauthorised systems and anti-virus to block programs that seek to steal or destroy data. And these tools must be automatically updated, as new viruses are released every day.

// FAMILY FRIENDLY FILTERS

The Communications Alliance, a communications industry forum in Australia, recommends Family Friendly Filters.

To be classified as a Family Friendly Filter, a filter undergoes independent testing to ensure it is effective, easy to use and that it is updated as and when required by the office of the eSafety Commisioner.

For example, if it determines that a specific website is prohibited under Australian law, a Family Friendly Filter will be updated by the filter company to block access to that website. All internet service providers must offer a Family Friendly Filter.

The office of the eSafety Commisioner has a series of filter classification codes to help parents decide what level or category of filter is appropriate for their household:

Unclassified – These filters block websites on the eSafety Commissioner's prohibited URL filter (PUF) list, and are recommended for 18-plus years of age

Class 1 – recommended for children over 15 years;

Class 2 – recommended for children between 10 and 15 years;

Class 3 – recommended for children under 10 years.

CURRENT APPROVED FAMILY FRIENDLY FILTERS ARE:

Norton Family Premier // **Version: 3.6.4.71**
Manufacturer: Symantec.
Class of accreditation: Recommended for children over 15 years of age (accreditation class 1).

Family Zone
Manufacturer: Family Zone.
Class of accreditation: Recommended for children under 10 years of age and older (accreditation class 3).

Australian Private Networks
Manufacturer: Australian Private Networks.
Class of accreditation: Recommended for children over 15 years of age (accreditation class 1).

Go to // **www.commsalliance.com.au/Activities/ispi/fff**

DEVICE ADVICE

Some nuts-and-bolts advice for managing your child's smartphone.

Major smartphone manufacturers and telephone service providers have a raft of tools and processes that you can use to take greater control of how your child uses their smartphone. If your child is under 18, then parents have most likely signed their mobile phone contract on their behalf, which gives them the right to know how their teenager is using that smartphone. Concerned parents can also place restrictions and limits on what content teens can see, what apps they can use and how much time they can spend online using their smartphone.

When you buy a smartphone for your child, go to the appropriate support centre website, such as the Apple support website or the online support centres for Samsung and Huawei, and find out what restrictions you can install before you hand over the phone to your teen.

Here we outline the basics for three popular smartphone brands.

*** Mobile Vendor Market Share Australia April 2019 by Global Stats

AT A GLANCE // APPLE DEVICES

- Instructions for setting up parental controls on Apple devices are found at www.apple.com/au/support/ Look for 'parental control'.
- You can restrict access to Safari, Camera, FaceTime, iTunes and iBooks stores, In-App Purchases, Siri, AirDrop, CarPlay and Installing and Deleting apps.
- You can prevent access to ratings (select the country in the ratings section to apply appropriate content ratings for that region), music and podcasts, movies, TV shows, books, apps, Siri and websites.
- You can prevent anyone from changing privacy settings including location services, contacts, calendars, reminders, photos, Bluetooth sharing, Twitter, Facebook and advertising.
- You can restrict features within Game Center, multiplayer games and adding friends.
- You can also adjust the time needed before a password is required to purchase content.
- AirDrop allows people to share and receive photos and documents from other nearby Apple iPhones and iPads. Set to Contacts Only to control who can see your child's iPhone and go to Receiving Off so they can't be sent any material.

HOW TO TURN ON RESTRICTIONS ON APPLE DEVICES

You can also turn on or enforce Restrictions using a profile (typically installed when using the device for business or education purposes). Check for installed profiles in Settings > General > Profiles. For additional information, contact the administrator or the person who installed the profile.

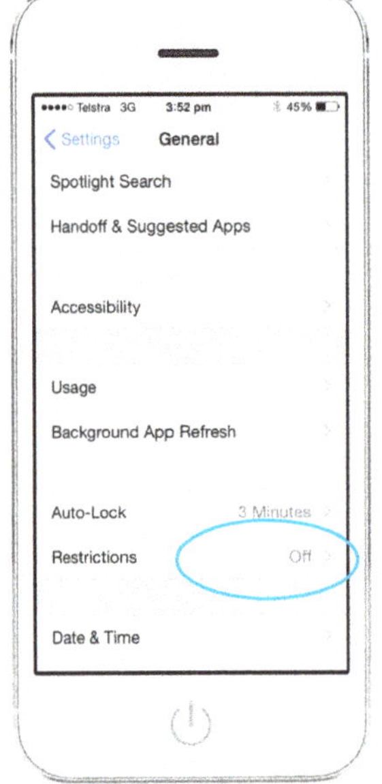

Photo: Thinkstock

TURN ON AND ADJUST RESTRICTIONS ON YOUR DEVICE

1 Tap Settings > General

2 Tap Enable Restrictions and enter a passcode

You'll need the passcode to change your settings or turn off Restrictions.

IMPORTANT NOTE

If you lose or forget your Restrictions passcode, you'll need to perform a factory restore to remove it.

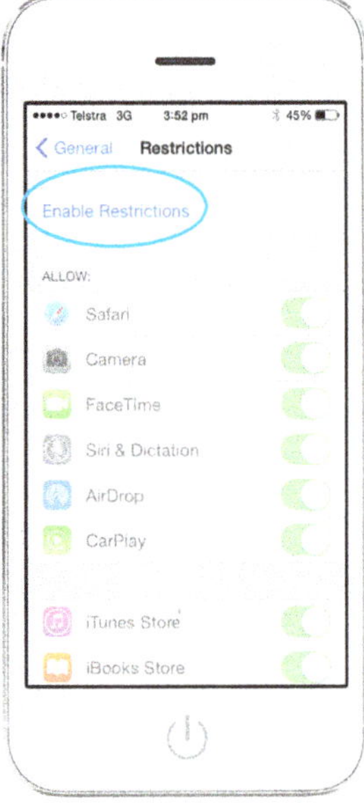

- Huawei has a Digital Balance feature that has parental controls to monitor a child's phone usage. Go to Settings, open Digital Balance and then enable screen time management. Then select the 'this is my kid's phone' option. Tap Next to set a daily screen time for your child. The screen time limit can only be increased with parental approval.
- You can also set a bedtime option for your child. You can configure the phone so the screen turns grey and apps can't be opened after bedtime.
- The Digital Balance option is also designed to help parents use their smartphone in a smarter way. It measures how much time you spend on your phone and how long you use various apps. You can also set time limits for yourself.

AT A GLANCE // SAMSUNG

- Samsung Parental Control allows parents to restrict the people your child can call or message and disable access to the web. You can also disable the camera feature. Instructions for setting up parental controls are found at **www.samsung.com/au/support/category/mobile/mobiledevice**
- To enable Parental Control from the Home menu screen, touch the Main menu tab.
- Touch Settings, scroll to Parental Controls and touch On.
- Enter a new code and then touch Done. Re-enter the new code, then touch Done again.
- Touch Restriction and touch On to access Voice, Messaging, Web Browser and Camera restrictions.
- To restrict contacts that your child can call, touch Allowed Numbers, touch Tap to add, and touch the contact name.
- To restrict who can be messaged, touch Allowed Numbers, touch Tap to add and touch the contact name to allow your child to message that person.
- With the Web Browser, touch On to disable access to the internet and go to Camera and touch On to disable access to the Camera.
- Press the Home key to return to the main Home screen menu.
- For younger mobile users, Samsung has a Kids Mode app that you can install on a child's mobile. Turn on Kids Mode, set up a profile for your child, secure it with a PIN, select which applications or features your child can access and then select Finish.

THE EDUCATOR

Steve Biddulph is a parent educator, psychologist and author. His books include *10 Things Girls Need Most*, *Raising Boys*, *Raising Girls* and *The New Manhood*.

Q. HOW IS MODERN LIFE MAKING THINGS MORE CHALLENGING FOR YOUNG PEOPLE TODAY?

A "We've put them in this frantic life with the hurry of our lives, the competitive nature of schooling and the way they see the world – it's just the contest. It's not just doing well at school, you have to look amazing and you have to be out there and switched on and then there's the 24/7 saturation of the internet … It's a perfect storm."

HOW DO PARENTS TALK ABOUT SEXTING AND SOME OF THE SEXUALISED IMAGERY CHILDREN SEE ON PHONES AND THE INTERNET?

A "Let kids know that you know about some of the things that they're encountering. Say, 'look, I'm sure people have shown you stuff on phones and pictures on the net that are pretty yucky looking, and I want to let you know that love and sex – that's not what it's really like. It's a really great part of life and we'll talk to you about that as time goes on and I'm always happy to talk about it'. Make those openings, so when some idiot holds a picture up in the playground that's gross, your daughter thinks 'mum knows about that so I don't have to keep that secret from her'. When kids are older you'd say something like what they need to know about pornography is that it's different – people in real life talk to each other and they're kind and not mean when they're having sex."

> "We can easily overreact or not know what to do because maybe we had parents who yelled at us and were cold and difficult."

WHAT DO PARENTS NEED TO BE AWARE OF ABOUT THEIR OWN BELIEFS AND EXPERIENCES WHEN DISCUSSING SENSITIVE TOPICS WITH CHILDREN?

A "What brings us unstuck as parents are the things we're just not quite aware of. So if a child is experiencing a little bit of bullying and we had bullying in our past, it's very hard to come to that in a steady, balanced way. We can easily overreact or not know what to do because maybe we had parents who yelled at us and were cold and difficult. Or perhaps you can say to yourself, 'my parents never helped me with sexuality so I'm going to have to get a bit of support for this and I want to do it differently'."

YOU HAVE WRITTEN EXTENSIVELY ABOUT BOYS AND THEIR HEALTH, WHAT ARE YOUR CONCERNS FOR GIRLS?

A "There may be people who've got daughters who are relaxed and confident and spirited into their mid-teens. They may have loyal friends and are treated respectfully by boys … but for about two girls out of five, that's just not so. They're massively anxious and currently across the Western world one in five teenage girls is on anxiety medication… Anxiety then drives the other things like self-harm and eating disorders and alcohol over-use and risky sex – but anxiety we think is the core."

HOW DO WE SUPPORT YOUNG PEOPLE, PARTICULARLY GIRLS, WHEN THEY FACE PROBLEMS WITH SOCIAL MEDIA?

A "Mothers and fathers have to wield a sword, and that might mean saying we don't have phones on after 7pm in our house, or we don't just leave the TV on all the time because our daughters will get this wash of completely unconscious imagery that if you're female you have to be thin and hot and sexy and young."

WHAT IS ONE THING PARENTS CAN DO TODAY TO TRY TO TACKLE THE SOCIAL MEDIA TSUNAMI THAT THEIR CHILDREN ARE EXPOSED TO?

A "Maybe have one night a week when you just hang out without a television – kids will just love it."

// STEVE BIDDULPH'S BOOKS

10 Things Girls Need Most

Raising Girls

Raising Boys

The New Manhood

Raising a Happy Child – in the precious years from birth to six

Raising Babies

The Making of Love

Love Laughter and Parenting

Stories of Manhood

// This is an edited interview conducted by Clare Bowditch with psychologist and author Steve Biddulph on ABC Radio Melbourne. www.stevebiddulph.com

FAMILY TECHNOLOGY USER AGREEMENT

I WILL KEEP MYSELF SAFE

- I will not give out any personal information, such as my age, last name, address or phone number, or meet someone I've met online, without my parents' permission.
- I will not put myself at risk by posting or sending inappropriate photos of myself or others.
- I will block creepy messages from people I don't know and inform my parents.
- I will tell my parents or an adult I trust if anything happens online that makes me feel uncomfortable, upset or sad.
- I will not share my password with anyone other than my parents, even my best friend.
- I will set privacy controls and always discuss with my parents when I want to create a social networking profile.

I WILL THINK FIRST

- I agree that not all apps, TV shows, movies, games, music and websites are right for me. I will talk to my parents if I am not sure what's appropriate.
- I will discuss ratings with my parents and agree to follow my family's agreed ratings.

The agreed ratings are:

____

____

- I know that not everything I read or see is true, and I will think about whether a source is credible.
- I agree not to download anything or fill out surveys without my parents' permission.
- I know that the pictures and videos I post online, and everything that I write about myself and my friends, will likely be online forever. Therefore I will not put anything on my profile that I wouldn't want my parents, teachers, or future employees to see.

I WILL BE A GOOD DIGITAL CITIZEN

- I agree not to bully anyone online by sending pictures or sharing videos without the permission of the person(s) in the photo/video, or by spreading gossip, setting up fake profiles or saying cruel things about people.
- I agree not to use technology to cheat on schoolwork and always cite the sources of information.
- I agree to flag and report content that is inappropriate and be an upstander against bullies by reporting incidents to trusted adults

I WILL KEEP A HEALTHY BALANCE

- Even though I love media, there are other things in my life that I'm interested in. So I will help my parents set time limits that make sense and then I will follow them.
- I will help my parents understand why media is so important to me by sharing my online experiences, but I also recognise that my safety is more important to them than anything else.
- The agreed charging time for all devices on a school night is 8pm.
- Our house will have a technology-free time for an hour each night for dinner.

The agreed time limits are:

____

____

____

____

IN EXCHANGE, MY PARENTS AGREE TO

- Recognise that media is a big part of my life, even if they don't always understand why.
- Before saying "no", talk with me about what worries them and why.
- Embrace my world: understand downloads, IM, online games and the sites that I like.

// SIGN SETUP

ME

....

MY PARENTS

....

// Kindly supplied by Paul Mears, director of Digital Learning, Firbank Grammar School.

ASSISTANCE

There are many places to get information and help.

// CYBER HELP

Office of the eSafety Commissioner
esafety.gov.au

Parent resources
www.esafety.gov.au/parents

Cyber help
www.staysmartonline.gov.au

Project Rockit
www.projectrockit.com.au

ThinkUKnow online advice
www.thinkuknow.org.au

ACORN cyber-crime reporting
www.acorn.gov.au

Gaming resources
www.videogames.org.au

Gaming workshops
www.instituteofgames.com

Online safety
www.internetsafeeducation.com

Protecting kids online
www.familyzone.com

Australian Council on Children and the Media app reviews
childrenandmedia.org.au/app-reviews

GameAware
www.gameaware.com.au

Family friendly filters
www.commsalliance.com.au/Activities/ispi/fff

Internet Safe Education
www.internetsafeeducation.com

Connect Safely
www.connectsafely.org

Internet safety
www.wesnet.org.au

Parent Guides
parentguides.com.au/social-media-101

// SOCIAL MEDIA LAWS

ACT // **www.thinkuknow.org.au**

Northern Territory //
www.thinkuknow.org.au

NSW // Legal Aid NSW under-18s youth hotline
1800 101 810

Queensland // Queensland sexting laws
**www.qld.gov.au/law/crime-and-police/types-of-crime/naked-pics //
www.legalaid.qld.gov.au**

Tasmania // **www.justice.tas.gov.au**

Victoria // sexting laws
www.legalaid.vic.gov.au/find-legal-answers/sex-and-law/sexting-and-child-pornography

// GENERAL HELP

Anxiety Recovery Centre Victoria (has links to other states)
www.arcvic.org.au

Australian Psychological Society find a psychologist
www.psychology.org.au/FindaPsychologist

Beyond Blue
1300 22 4636
healthyfamilies.beyondblue.org.au

Black Dog Institute
www.blackdoginstitute.org.au

CAT Teams
www.health.vic.gov.au/mentalhealthservices/adult/

Health Direct services directory
www.healthdirect.gov.au

Mind Australia
1300 286 463
www.mindaustralia.org.au

Mind Health Connect parenting help
www.mindhealthconnect.org.au/parenting

Mind Matters
www.mindmatters.edu.au

Royal Australian College and New Zealand College of Psychiatrists find a psychiatrist
www.yourhealthinmind.org/find-a-psychiatrist

Raising Children Network // Australian parenting website
raisingchildren.net.au

Safe Schools Coalition Australia
www.safeschoolscoalition.org.au

Sane Australia
1800 18 7263
www.sane.org

Transcend (transgender support)
www.transcendsupport.com.au

National LGBTI Health Alliance
www.lgbtihealth.org.au

QLife
1800 184 527
www.qlife.org.au

Minus18
minus18.org.au

Suicide Call Back Service
1300 659 467 //
www.suicidecallbackservice.org.au

// YOUNG PEOPLE

ReachOut
au.reachout.com

Alannah & Madeline Foundation // Anti-bullying
www.amf.org.au

Headspace // Youth mental health
www.headspace.org.au

Kids Helpline
1800 55 1800
www.kidshelpline.com.au

Rosie // Research-based information for girls
 www.rosie.org.au

The Line // Relationships advice for young people
www.theline.org.au
Youth Beyond Blue // Beyond Blue's youth program
www.youthbeyondblue.com

// GAMBLING

Gambler's Help Youthline (24/7)
1800 262 376

Gambling Help Online
www.gamblinghelponline.org.au

Parent resources
 www.responsiblegambling.vic.gov.au

KidBet
kidbet.com.au

// APPS AND ONLINE TOOLS

MOOD DISORDER APPS VIA REACHOUT
au.professionals.reachout.com/apps-and-online-tools/mood-disorders

ANXIETY DISORDER APPS VIA REACHOUT
au.professionals.reachout.com/apps-and-online-tools/anxiety-disorders

TOOLS FOR GENERAL WELL-BEING VIA REACHOUT
au.professionals.reachout.com/apps-and-online-tools/wellbeing-apps-and-tools

REACHOUT WELL-BEING TOOLBOX
au.reachout.com/sites/thetoolbox

BEACON 2.0. PORTAL FOR ONLINE MENTAL AND PHYSICAL DISORDER APPLICATIONS
www.beacon.anu.edu.au

// PARENT HELP LINES

ACT // **(02) 6287 3833**	Queensland // **1300 301 300**
Northern Territory // **1300 301 300**	Tasmania // **1300 808 178**
NSW // **1300 1300 52**	Victoria // **13 22 89**
South Australia // **1300 364 100**	Western Australia // **1800 654 432**